EARTH'S LANDFORMS

MOUNTAINS

by Lisa J. Amstutz

Raintree is an imprint of Capstone Global Library Limited, a company incorporated in England and Wales having its registered office at 264 Banbury Road, Oxford, OX2 7DY – Registered company number: 6695582

www.raintree.co.uk
myorders@raintree.co.uk

Text © Capstone Global Library Limited 2021
The moral rights of the proprietor have been asserted.

Edited by Alesha Sullivan
Designed by Bobbie Nuytten
Original illustrations © Capstone Global Library Limited 2021
Picture research by Kelly Garvin
Production by Tori Abraham
Originated by Capstone Global Library Ltd

978 1 3982 0280 1 (hardback)
978 1 3982 0279 5 (paperback)

British Library Cataloguing in Publication Data
A full catalogue record for this book is available from the British L

Acknowledgements
We would like to thank the following for permission to reproduce photographs: Capstone Press/ Karon Dubke, 21; Shutterstock: alsem, 17 (bottom), Andrea Danti, 7, Andrei Stepanov, 17 (top), Creative Travel Projects, back cover, epicureyka, 19, fboudrias, 9, Gaspar Janos, 5, iamnong, cover, kavram, 13 (t), Niti Thanomsri, 13 (b), Protasov AN, 15 (t), Randy McVeigh, 15 (b), Vixit, 11

Printed and bound in India

Contents

Words in **bold** are in the glossary.

WHAT IS A MOUNTAIN?

Have you ever seen a mountain? You probably had to look up! Many mountains reach high up in the air. A mountain is taller than a hill. Mountains come in many sizes and shapes. Some are round or flat on top. Others have pointy **peaks**. A group of mountains is called a **range**.

HOW ARE MOUNTAINS MADE?

Mountains are made in different ways. Under your feet, there is a lot going on. Big rocky **plates** are below the ground. These plates move on top of melted rock. Sometimes the plates crash into each other. The land rises up and makes a mountain.

Below ground, rocky plates
move on top of melted rock.

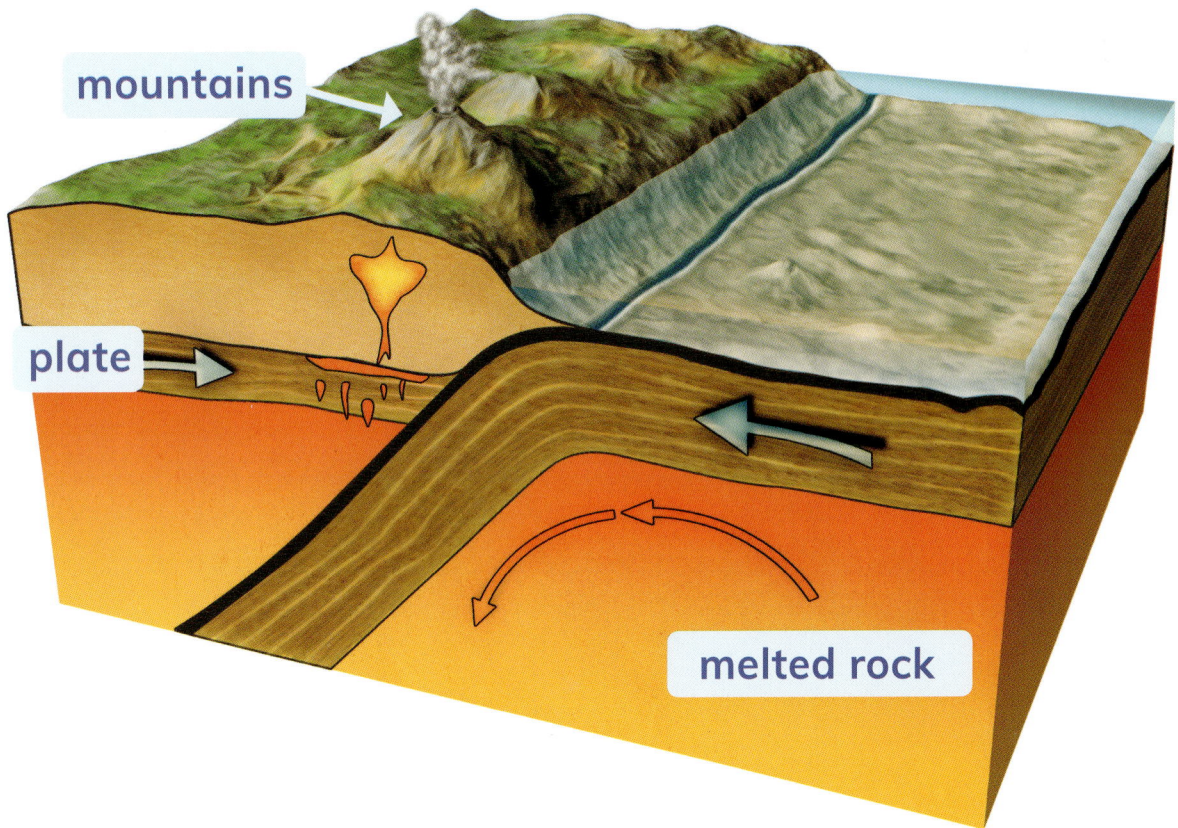

mountains

plate

melted rock

Volcanoes can make mountains too. Hot liquid called **lava** comes out of a volcano. It flows over land. It cools and hardens into rock.

The lava builds up and makes a mountain. Volcanoes can be found under the sea. The part above water becomes an **island**.

WHERE ARE MOUNTAINS FOUND?

Mountains are found all over the world. Some are on land. Others are deep in the sea. South America has the longest mountain range.

The Himalayas in Asia is a range that has Mount Everest. It is the tallest mountain in the world. It is more than 8,839 metres (29,000 feet) high!

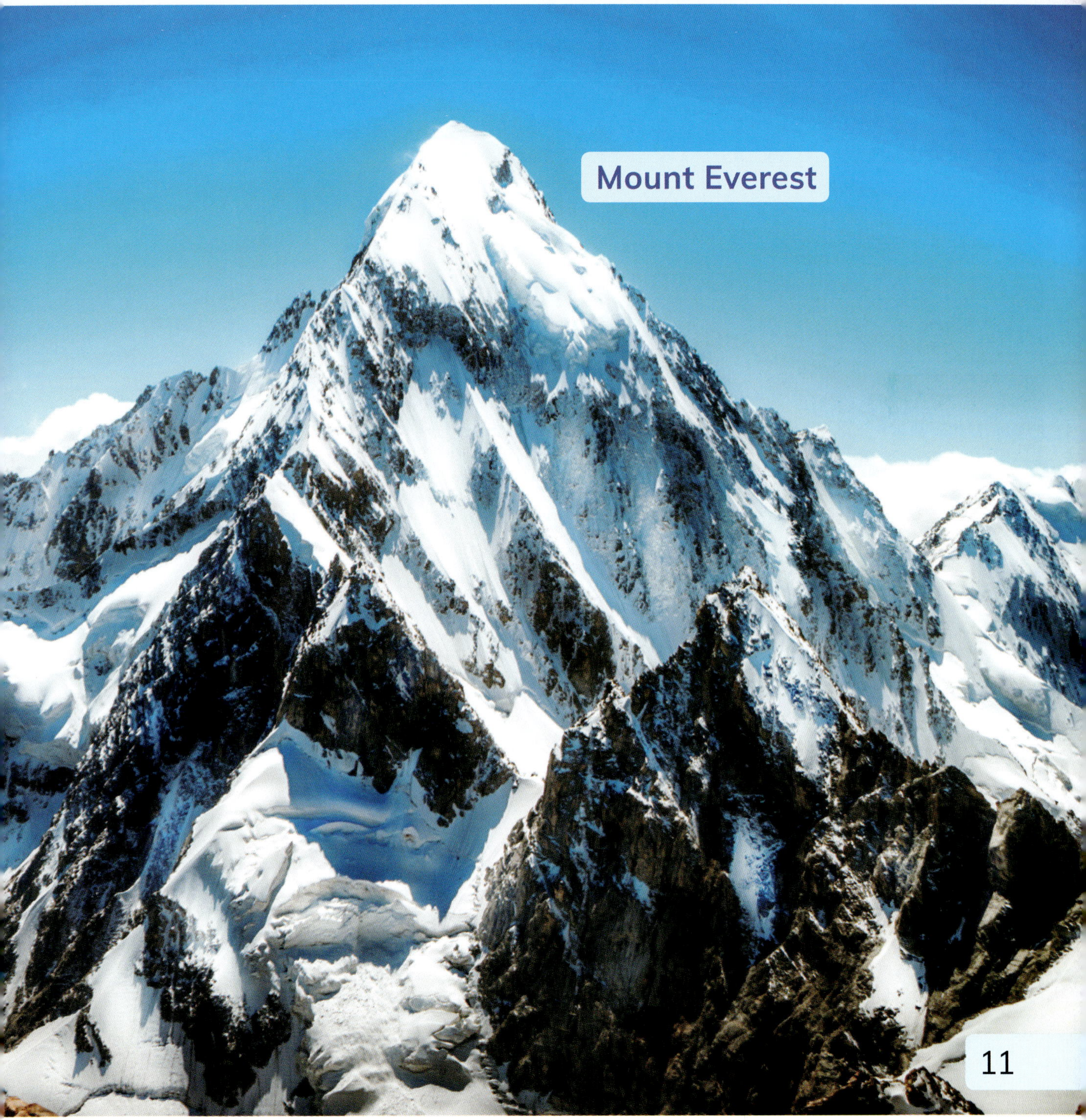
Mount Everest

CHANGING MOUNTAINS

Mountains change over time.
Wind and water wear away the rock.
They can flatten mountain tops.

As air rises over a mountain, it cools.
The water in the air falls as rain or snow.
It is colder at the top of a mountain than
at the bottom.

WHAT LIVES ON A MOUNTAIN?

Animals live on mountains. Many are good at climbing. Bears and bighorn sheep live on mountains. Mountain lions do too. Mountain goats climb **steep** mountain cliffs.

mountain goat

Look up! Birds make nests on the sides of mountains. Watch out below! Snakes hide in the rocks.

High up, there are few trees. Grasses and bushes grow low to the ground. Some can even live under the snow.

Many people live in areas where there are mountains. Some live right on a mountain! Others just like to climb them. Would you like to climb a mountain?

Make a mountain

You can make a mountain of your own!

You'll need:

- pile of tea towels
- two large books

Instructions:

1. Stack the tea towels on top of one another.

2. Place one book on each end.

3. Push the books towards each other. The books are like plates in Earth's crust. They crash into each other. The towels push up, just like a mountain does.

Glossary

island piece of land that is surrounded by water

lava hot, liquid rock that pours out of a volcano when it erupts

peak pointed top of an island or mountain

plate large sheet of rock that is a piece of Earth's crust

range large group of mountains

steep having a sharp slope or slant

volcano opening in Earth's surface that sometimes sends out hot lava, steam and ash

Find out more

Books

Exploring Mountains (Exploring Habitats with Benjamin Blog and His Inquisitive Dog), Anita Ganeri (Raintree, 2015)

Mountains and Valleys (Let's Explore Britain), James Nixon (Raintree, 2018)

Websites

www.bbc.com/bitesize/articles/z4g3qp3
Learn more about mountains and how they are formed.

www.dkfindout.com/uk/earth/mountains
Find out more about mountains.

Index